The ABCs of Dare...

May All Your Dares Come True

HAZELDEN

Keep Coming Back™

CREATED BY MEIJI STEWART

ABC Writings © Meiji Stewart
Graphic Design & Illustration by Jeff Kahn
Graphic Production by Darryl Yee

The ABCs of Dare to...

© 2001 by Meiji Stewart

All rights reserved. Written permission to reprint the ABC writings must be secured from Meiji Stewart. Permission for all other quotations must be secured from the publisher except for brief quotations in critical reviews or articles.

ISBN 1-56838-744-X

Hazelden
P.O. Box 176
15251 Pleasant Valley Road
Center City, MN 55012-0176
1-800-328-9000
www.hazelden.org

05 04 03 02 01   6 5 4 3 2 1
ABC writings ©Meiji Stewart • Visit www.abcwritings.com

Thank you to Bette Trono and the publishing committee ©Portal Publications for permission to use the cover illustration.
www.portalpub.com

DEDICATED TO:

Marshall B. Rosenberg, the founder of the Center for Nonviolent Communication (CNVC) and to all those around the world who help share his message. Rosenberg's language of compassion has significantly improved the quality of my personal (especially with myself) and professional relationships. CNVC has also increased the clarity and consciousness with which I use language and strengthened my intention to live a loving and compassionate life. Please visit *www.cnvc.org* for more information about his work.

THANKS TO:

Jeff Kahn for the great book cover and interior page designs. Please visit him at *www.kahn-design.com* to see his wonderful designs and illustrations. Darryl Yee for his great production work and help with some of the interior illustrations. Neill Gibson, who is the passionate driving force behind PuddleDancer's promotion of Marshall Rosenberg's book *Nonviolent Communication*. Visit *www.nonviolentcommunication.com* for more information.

I also want to say thank you to my best friend and wife, Claudia, my daughter, Malia, my stepson, Tommy, my parents, Richard and Nannette, my sister, Leslie, my brothers, Ray and Scott, my nephews and nieces, Sebastien, Emilie, Skye, Luke, Jake, Jessie Nannette, Cairo, and Kamana, and to Richard, Jewels, Tom, Fumi, Jocelyne, and Stephen, and my father-in-law, Jim, and not forgetting, of course, our two greyhounds, Zoie and Sunset, and our two cats, Oliver and Tito.

Dare to...

Ask for what you want
Believe in yourself
Change your mind
Do what you love
Enjoy each and every day
Follow your heart's desire
Give more than you receive
Have a sense of humor
Insist on being yourself
Join in more
Kiss and make up
Love and be loved
Make new friends

Nurture your spirit
Overcome adversity
Play more
Question conformity
Reach for the stars
Speak your truth
Take personal responsibility
Understand more, judge less
Volunteer your time
Walk through fear
Xperience the moment
Yearn for grace
be Zany

© 2001 Meiji Stewart

Dare to...

A$k

For What You Want

Dare to…Ask For What You Want

> *You have got to know what it is you want! Or someone is going to sell you a bill of goods somewhere along the line that will do irreparable damage to your self-esteem, your sense of worth, and your stewardship of talents that God gave you.*
>
> ~Richard Nelson Bolles

> *The first principle of success is desire—
> knowing what you want.
> Desire is the planting of your seed.*
>
> ~Robert Collier

Dare to…Ask For What You Want

Many things are lost for want of asking.
~English proverb

*You can have anything you want if
you want it desperately enough.
You must want it with an inner exuberance
that erupts through the skin
and joins the energy that created the world.*

~Sheilah Graham

Dare to…Ask For What You Want

> *Loving yourself means giving your body the food, exercise and rest that it needs. It means listening to your feelings and asking others for what you want– without feeling guilty about it.*
>
> ~Douglas Bloch

> *The starting point of all achievement is desire. Keep this constantly in mind. Weak desires bring weak results, just as a small amount of fire makes a small amount of heat.*
>
> ~Napoleon Hill

Dare to…Ask For What You Want

*All I know is I feel won't
when I'm told to do a don't.*

~Ruth Bebermeyer

*Thinking about what you don't want to happen
increases the odds that it will.*

~Robert Kriegel

*When we speak, the clearer we are about what
we are wanting back, the more likely we are to get it.*

~Marshall B. Rosenberg

*If you really want something,
you can figure out how to make it happen.*

~Cher

It seems to me we can never give up longing and wishing while we are thoroughly alive. There are certain things we feel to be beautiful and good, and we must hunger after them.

~George Eliot

Dare to...

Believe

In Yourself

Dare to…Believe In Yourself

> *You are one of a kind;
> therefore, no one can really predict
> to what heights you might soar.
> Even you will not know
> until you spread your wings!*
>
> ~Gil Atkinson

> *No matter what age you are,
> or what your circumstances might be,
> you are special and still have something unique to offer.
> Your life, because of who you are, has meaning.*
>
> ~Barbara De Angelis

Dare to…Believe In Yourself

Everyone has inside of him a piece of good news.
The good news is that you don't know how great you can be!
How much you can love! What you can accomplish!
And what your potential is!

~Anne Frank

Remember that you are unique.
If that is not fulfilled,
then something wonderful has been lost.

~Martha Graham

You are here for a purpose.
There is no duplicate of you in the whole wide world.
There never has been. There never will be.
You were brought here now to fill a certain need.
Take time to think that over.

~Lou Astin

If we did all the things we are capable of,
we would literally astound ourselves.

~Thomas Edison

The ABCs of You Are...

Amazing, the architect of your destiny.

Beautiful, both inside and out.

Courageous, being true to yourself.

Dynamic, ever changing and growing.

Enthusiastic, about living and loving life.

Fallible, perfectly imperfect.

Grateful, for each and every day.

Healthy, full of energy.

Intuitive, looking within for guidance.

Joyful, happy to be you.

Kindhearted, reaching out to others.

Lovable, exactly as you are.

Miraculous, a child of the universe.

Now here, fully in this moment.

Optimistic, anything is possible.

Powerful, beyond imagination.

Quick to build bridges not walls.

Resourceful, obstacles are stepping-stones.

Spiritual, having a human experience.

Trustworthy, speaking from your heart.

Unique and unrepeatable.

Valuable, you make a difference.

Wise, open to all of life's lessons.

Xcited, about pursuing your dreams.

Young at heart, delightfully childlike.

Zany and have a great sense of humor.

©Meiji Stewart

At bottom every man knows well enough that he is a unique being, only once on this earth; and by no extraordinary chance will such a marvelously picturesque piece of diversity in unity as he is, ever be put together a second time.

~Friedrich Wilhelm Nietzsche

You are child of the universe, no less than the trees and the stars; you have a right to be here. And whether or not it is clear to you, no doubt the universe is unfolding as it should.

~Max Ehrmann

Dare to...

Change
Your Mind

*Take out your brain and jump on it–
it gets all caked up.*

~Mark Twain

*Do I contradict myself?
Very well then, I contradict myself
(I am large, I contain multitudes).*

~Walt Whitman

I am committed to truth, not consistency.

~Mahatma Gandhi

*If you keep doing what you've always done,
you'll keep getting what you've always got.*

~Peter Francisco

*Any path is only a path. There is no affront to oneself
or others in dropping it if that is what your heart tells you.*

~Carlos Castaneda

*My mind is made up;
don't try to confuse me with the facts.*

~Author unknown

*If my mind ever listened to what my mouth said,
I'd have a lot of accounting to do.*

~Steve Allen

*Faced with the choice between changing one's mind
and proving there is no need to do so,
almost everyone gets busy on the proof.*

~John Kenneth Galbraith

Nurture your mind with great thoughts.

~Benjamin Disraeli

Change your thoughts, and you change your world.

~Norman Vincent Peale

No matter how far you have gone on a wrong road, turn back.

~Turkish proverb

Dare to…Change Your Mind

One night at sea, a ship's captain saw what he
thought were the lights of another ship heading toward him.
He had his signalman blink to the other ship,
"Change your course ten degrees south."
The reply came back, "Change your course ten degrees north."
The ship's captain answered, "I am the captain. Change your course south."
Another reply came back, "Well, I'm a seaman first class.
Change your course north."
The captain was mad now.
"I said change your course south. I'm on a battleship!"
To which the reply came back,
"And I say change your course north. I'm in a lighthouse."

~Author unknown

Dare to...

Do
What You Love

Do what you love. Know your own bone.
Gnaw at it, bury it, unearth it, and gnaw it still.

~Henry David Thoreau

Do what you love and the money will follow.

~Marsha Sinetar

Winning the Nobel Prize in physics wasn't half as exciting
as doing the work itself.

~Maria Goeppert-Mayer

*If you find out what it is you love to do and
give your whole life to it, then there is no contradiction,
and in that state your being is your doing.*

~Jiddu Krishnamurti

*To love what you do and feel that it matters–
how could anything be more fun?*

~Katherine Graham

Dare to…Do What You Love

*N*ever cut loose from your longings.

~Amos Oz

*F*ollow your own bent, no matter what people say.

~Karl Marx

*C*hoose a job you love,
and you will never have to work a day in your life.

~Confucius

You are the one person for whom you are entirely responsible. Your world, your life can be better only if you make it so. As you improve yourself, you influence all others around you. Keep in mind that you came into this life with a purpose to perform.

~Harold Sherman

*Cherish your visions, your ideals,
the music that stirs in your heart.
If you remain true to them, your world
will at last be built.*

~James Allen

To find in ourselves what makes life worth living is risky business, for it means that once we know we must seek it. It also means that without it life will be valueless.

~Marsha Sinetar

We must create our own world.

~Louise Nevelson

Discover your possibilities.

~Dr. Robert Schuller

Dare to...

Enjoy

Each And Every Day

Dare to…Enjoy Each And Every Day

> *This is the best day the world has ever seen.*
> *Tomorrow will be better.*
>
> ~R. A. Campbell

> *When shall we live if not now?*
>
> ~M. F. K. Fisher

> *Each day comes bearing its gifts. Untie the ribbons.*
>
> ~Ann Schabacker

*Yesterday is but a dream, tomorrow is only a vision.
But today well lived makes every yesterday a dream of
happiness and every tomorrow a vision of hope. Look well,
therefore, to this day, for it is life, the very life of life.*

~Sanskrit proverb

One today is worth two tomorrows.

~Benjamin Franklin

Dare to…Enjoy Each And Every Day

$\mathcal{A}$ *man should hear a little music, read a little poetry, and see a fine picture every day of his life, in order that worldly cares may not obliterate the sense of the beautiful which God has implanted in the human soul.*

~Johann von Goethe

$\mathcal{N}$*ormal day, let me be aware of the treasure you are.*

~Author unknown

The ABCs of Things to Do Today…

Act from your heart.

Believe in possibilities.

Count your blessings.

Do something for others.

Enjoy yourself.

Find everyday magic.

Give encouragement.

Have a sense of adventure.

Inspire with compassion.

Jettison judgments.

Keep an open mind.

Live from the inside out.

Mend a quarrel.

Nurture friendships.

Overcome adversity.

Progress not perfection.

Quiet your mind.

Remember "it's all good."

Say "I love you."

Take care of business.

Use your time wisely.

Volunteer and give back.

Work up a sweat.

Xplore, dream, and discover.

Yodel more, yawn less.

Zest to make memories.

©Meiji Stewart

Dare to…Enjoy Each And Every Day

> *People are always asking about the good old days.*
> *I say, why don't you say the good "now" days?*
> *Isn't "now" the only time you're living?*

~Robert M. Young

> *It is only possible to live happily ever after*
> *on a day to day basis.*

~Margaret Bonnano

Dare to...

Follow
Your Heart's Desire

Dare to…Follow Your Heart's Desire

> *If I have the belief that I can do it,*
> *I shall surely acquire the capacity to do it*
> *even if I may not have it at the beginning.*
>
> ~Mahatma Gandhi

> *Make no little plans; they have no magic to stir men's blood.*
> *Make big plans, aim high in hope and work.*
>
> ~Daniel H. Burnham

> *To try is to risk failure. But risk must be taken,*
> *as the greatest hazard in life is to risk nothing.*
> *The person who risks nothing, does nothing,*
> *has nothing, and is nothing.*
>
> ~Author unknown

Am I willing to give up what I have in order to be what I am not yet?...
Am I able to follow the spirit of love into the desert?...
It is a frightening and sacred moment.
There is no return. One's life is changed forever.
It is the fire that gives us our shape.

~Mary Caroline Richards

Far away there in the sunshine are my highest aspirations.
I may not reach them, but I can look up and see their beauty,
believe in them and try to follow where they may lead.

~Louisa May Alcott

Dare to…Follow Your Heart's Desire

We must dare, and dare again, and go on daring.

~Georges Jacques Danton

*People are afraid of the future, of the unknown.
If a man faces up to it, and takes the dare of the future,
he can have some control over his destiny.
That's an exciting idea to me, better than waiting with
everybody else to see what's going to happen.*

~John Glenn

Dare to…Follow Your Heart's Desire

I'm in love with the potential of miracles.
For me, the safest place is out on a limb.

~Shirley MacLaine

Risk! Risk anything! Care no more for the opinion of others,
for those voices. Do the hardest thing on earth for you.
Act for yourself. Face the truth.

~Katherine Mansfield

Why not go out on a limb? Isn't that where the fruit is?

~Frank Scully

What we vividly imagine, ardently desire, enthusiastically act upon, must inevitably come to pass.

~Colin P. Sisson

It's time to start living the life we've imagined.

~Henry James

Dare to...

Give
More Than You Receive

Dare to…Give More Than You Receive

*The best thing about giving of ourselves is that
what we get is always better than what we give.
The reaction is greater than the action.*

~Orison Swett Marden

*The greatest gifts we can give to others
are not material things but gifts of ourselves.
The great gifts are those of love, of inspiration, of kindness,
of encouragement, of forgiveness, of ideas and ideals.*

~Author unknown

Dare to…Give More Than You Receive

Give me the ready hand rather than the ready tongue.

~Giuseppe Gabribaldi

Kindness in giving creates love.

~Lao-Tzu

He who obtains has little. He who scatters has much.

~Lao-Tzu

*It's not how much we give
but how much love we put into giving.*

~Mother Teresa

Dare to…Give More Than You Receive

God has blessed each of us in different, beautiful and special ways. When we share ourselves with others, we give gifts of love, friendship and caring. In this way we help feed the hungry, clothe the naked and comfort the lonely and ill. We become friends. When we do these things, we often find we are blessed as much as, and perhaps more than, those we help.

~Shirley Pieters Vogel

The miracle is this–the more we share, the more we have.

~Leonard Nimoy

Dare to…Give More Than You Receive

*To give a gift of one's self is a manifestation of love.
It is when you reveal yourself nakedly and honestly,
at any given moment, for no other purpose than as a gift of
what's alive in you. Not to blame, criticize, or punish.
Just "Here I am, and here is what I would like."
This is my vulnerability at this moment.
To me, that is a way of manifesting love.*

~Marshall B. Rosenberg

*I have found that there is a tremendous joy in giving.
It is a very important part of the joy of living.*

~William Black

Dare to…Give More Than You Receive

> *When someone steals another's clothes, we call him a thief.*
> *Should we not give the same name to one*
> *who could clothe the naked and does not?*
> *The bread in your cupboard belongs to the hungry;*
> *the coat hanging unused in your closet*
> *belongs to the one who needs it;*
> *the shoes rotting in your closet*
> *belong to the one who has no shoes;*
> *the money which you hoard up belongs to the poor.*

~St. Basil the Great

> *For it is in giving that we receive.*

~St. Francis of Assisi

Dare to...

Have
A Sense Of Humor

Dare to…Have A Sense Of Humor

*If you wear a rubber nose for a week,
your life will be changed
because you will get in touch with
the joy you can bring to the world.*

~Dr. Hunter "Patch" Adams

*Do not take life too seriously.
You will never get out of it alive.*

~Elbert Hubbard

I realize that a sense of humor isn't for everyone.
It's only for people who want to have fun,
enjoy life, and feel alive.

~Anne Wilson Schaef

If lawyers are disbarred and clergymen defrocked,
doesn't it follow that electricians can be delighted;
musicians denoted; cowboys deranged;
models deposed; tree surgeons debarked;
and dry cleaners depressed?

~Virginia Ostman

Dare to…Have A Sense Of Humor

I never lose sight of the fact that just being is fun.

~Katharine Hepburn

*Imagination was given to man
to compensate him for what he is not,
and a sense of humor was provided
to console him for what he is.*

~Robert Walpole

Dare to…Have A Sense Of Humor

Work, work, work and more work is do-do.
Work and relax, work and relax is do-be-do.

~Dr. Richard Diamond

If you're too busy to laugh, you're too busy, period.

~Janet Meyer

Warning: Humor is hazardous to your illness.

~Ellie Katz

Dare to…Have A Sense Of Humor

You can only be as good as you dare to be bad.

~John Barrymore

*Life does not cease to be funny when people die
any more than it ceases to be serious when people laugh.*

~George Bernard Shaw

*Don't take yourself too seriously.
And don't be too serious about
not taking yourself too seriously.*

~Howard Ogden

Dare to...

Insist
On Being Yourself

Dare to…Insist On Being Yourself

The privilege of a lifetime is being who you are.

~Joseph Campbell

Everyone has their own specific vocation or mission in life. Therein, we cannot be replaced, nor can our lives be repeated. Thus, everyone's task is as unique as their specific opportunity to implement it.

~Victor Frankl

Our main task is to give birth to ourselves.

~Erich Fromm

Be yourself. Who else is better qualified?

~Frank J. Giblin II

If no one heeds your call, go forth alone.

~Maharishi Mahesh Yogi

Dare to…Insist On Being Yourself

> *If a man does not keep pace with his companions,*
> *perhaps it is because he hears a different drummer.*
> *Let him step to the music which he hears,*
> *however measured or far away.*
>
> ~Henry David Thoreau

> *God made no two people exactly alike because*
> *He had a different idea for each of us.*
> *To the extent that we live that idea,*
> *we are fulfilling our purpose on earth.*
>
> ~Alan Cohen

Dare to…Insist On Being Yourself

*Of all the people you will know in a lifetime,
you are the only one you will never leave nor lose.
To the question of your life, you are the only answer.
To the problems of your life, you are the only solution.*

~Jo Coudert

*Something wonderful, something hidden.
A gift unique to you. Find it.*

~Ralph Waldo Emerson

Dare to…Insist On Being Yourself

> *What matters is what you think about yourself.*
> *You must find the part in life that fits*
> *and then give up acting;*
> *your profession is being.*
>
> ~Quentin Crisp

> *Some people march to a different drummer–*
> *and some people polka.*
>
> ~Author unknown

Dare to...

Join
In More

Dare to…Join In More

*We are all dependent on one another,
every soul of us on earth.*

~George Bernard Shaw

*No man is an island, entire of itself;
every man is a piece of the continent, a part of man.*

~John Donne

Nobody, but nobody, can make it out here alone.

~Maya Angelou

Dare to…Join In More

Alone we can so do little; together we can do so much.

~Helen Keller

Never doubt that a small group of thoughtful, committed people can change the world. Indeed, it is the only thing that ever has.

~Margaret Mead

*Fortify yourself with a flock of friends! You can select them
at random, write to one, dine with one, visit one,
or take your problems to one. There is always at least one
who will understand, inspire, and give you
the lift you may need at the time.*

~George Mathew Adams

*What a world this would be
if we just built bridges instead of walls.*

~Carlos Ramirez

The ABCs of Life Are...

an *A*rt not a science

*B*rief, so do what you love

a *C*hoice, don't let it pass you by

a *D*ance, do the twist, not the tiptoe

*E*lementary, keep it simple

*F*ragile, handle with care

a *G*ift, unwrap "the present"

*H*ard, compared to what?

*I*nevitable, joy is optional

a *J*ourney, be kind to fellow travelers

*K*nowing, the best things aren't things

a *L*esson, everyone is a teacher

a *M*ystery, embrace the unknown

*N*ow, not a someday thing

*O*riginal, don't be a copy

a *P*arty, everyone is invited

a *Q*uestion, love is the answer

a *R*oller coaster, enjoy the ride

*S*ubject to change without notice

*T*oo important to take too seriously

*U*ncertain, enjoy each and every day

a *V*alentine, love and be loved

*W*hatever you decide it to be

an *X*perience to treasure

*Y*ummy, savor the flavor

*Z*any, remember to laugh

©Meiji Stewart

Empathy, requires focusing full attention on the other person's message. We give to others the time and space they need to express themselves fully and to feel understood.

~Marshall B. Rosenberg

Snowflakes, leaves, humans, plants, raindrops, stars, molecules, microscopic entities all come in communities. The singular cannot in reality exist.

~Paula Gunn Allen

Dare to...

Kiss
And Make Up

*All I can do is engage with complete sincerity.
Then, whatever happens, there is no regret.*

~Dalai Lama

*Look at each person you meet as a person in progress.
Then look in the mirror and see another person in progress.*

~Carl Rogers

Conflicts, even of long standing duration, can be resolved if people come out of their heads and stop criticizing and analyzing each other, and instead get in touch with their needs, and hear the needs of others, and realize the interdependence that we all have in relation to each other. We can't win at somebody else's expense. We can only fully be satisfied when the other person's needs are fulfilled as well as our own.

~Marshall B. Rosenberg

The old law of "an eye for an eye" leaves everybody blind.

~Martin Luther King Jr.

Dare to…Kiss And Make Up

People are lonely because they build walls instead of bridges.

~Joseph Fort Newton

*The ultimate test of a relationship is to disagree
but to hold hands.*

~Alexandra Penny

*No one on earth can hurt you,
unless you accept the hurt in your own mind. . . .
The problem is not other people; it is your reaction.*

~Vernon Howard

I do my thing, and you do your thing. I am not in this world to live up to your expectations and you are not in this world to live up to mine. You are you and I am I, and if by chance we find each other, it's beautiful. If not, it can't be helped.

~Frederick S. Perls

Everything is a gift of the universe—even joy, anger, jealousy, frustration, or separateness. Everything is perfect either for our growth or our enjoyment.

~Ken Keyes Jr.

*We create our own feelings by the thoughts we choose to think.
We have the ability to make different choices
and create different experiences.*

~Louise Hay

*Kissing is a means of getting two people so close together that
they can't see anything wrong with each other.*

~Rene Yasenek

Dare to...

Love
And Be Loved

Dare to…Love And Be Loved

> *Love everybody you love;
> you can never tell when they might not be there.*
>
> ~Nancy Bush Ellis

> *The Eskimos had fifty-two names for snow
> because snow was important to them;
> there ought to be as many for love.*
>
> ~Margaret Atwood

> *We are not held back by the love we didn't receive in the past,
> but by the love were not extending in the present.*
>
> ~Marianne Williamson

The ABCs of Love Are...

The *A*nswer, whatever the question.

*B*eing there, to wipe away the tears.

*C*hoice, color the world beautiful.

*D*oing, actions speak louder than words.

*E*verywhere, if you look for it.

*F*orgiving, and for giving.

*G*ratitude, for all that is, was, and will be.

*H*olding hands more, hurrying less.

*I*nclusive, not exclusive.

*J*ourneying together, on our own paths.

*K*indness, do what you can when you can.

*L*aughing, listening, and letting go.

*M*agical, the more you give, the more you receive.

*N*ow, why wait until tomorrow?

*O*pen-minded, there are many sides to every story.

*P*owerful, be the cause of wonderful things.

*Q*uick to build bridges and take down walls.

*R*ealizing, you wouldn't want it any other way.

*S*haring, dare to care.

*T*houghtful, tender, and true.

*U*nconditional, no ifs, ands, or buts.

*V*ital, like sunshine and rain to a flower.

*W*illingness, to see through the eyes of a child.

*X*pressing your truth, knowing the answers will come.

*Y*earning, for connection not correction.

*Z*any, dive deep into the mystery.

©Meiji Stewart

Dare to…Love And Be Loved

If we all discovered that we had only five minutes left to say all that we wanted to say, every telephone booth would be occupied by people calling other people to tell them that they loved them.

~Christopher Morley

Do not keep the alabaster boxes of your love and tenderness sealed up until your friends are dead. Fill their lives with sweetness. Speak approving, cheering words while their ears can hear them and while their hearts can be thrilled by them.

~Henry Ward Beecher

*There is no difficulty that enough love will not conquer;
no disease that enough love will not heal;
no door that enough love will not open. It makes no difference
how deeply seated may be the trouble; how hopeless the
outlook; how muddled the tangle; how great the mistake.
A sufficient realization of love will dissolve it all.
If only you could love enough you would be the happiest
and most powerful being in the world.*

~Emmet Fox

*Being with you is never quite long enough.
Seeing you is never quite soon enough.
Missing you is always there.*

~Claudia Faye Stewart

Dare to…Love And Be Loved

There is a universal truth that I have found in my work. Everybody longs to be loved. And the greatest thing we can do is let somebody know that they are loved and capable of loving.

~Fred Rogers

Everyone needs reminders that the fact of their being on this earth is important and that each life changes everything.

~Marge Kennedy

Dare to...

Make
New Friends

Dare to…Make New Friends

*Meeting someone for the first time is like going on a treasure hunt.
What wonderful worlds we can find in others!*

~Edward E. Ford

*My friends are an oasis to me, encouraging me to go on.
They are essential to my well-being.*

~Dee Brestin

*If you think it's hard to meet new people,
try picking up the wrong golf ball.*

~Jack Lemmon

Dare to…Make New Friends

You can make more friends in two months by becoming interested in other people than you can in two years by trying to get other people interested in you.

~Dale Carnegie

Animals are such agreeable friends— they ask no questions, they pass no criticisms.

~George Eliot

There is only one thing better than making a new friend, and that is keeping an old one.

~Elmer G. Leterman

Dare to…Make New Friends

If you make friends with yourself, you will never be alone.

~Maxwell Maltz

Oh, the comfort, the inexpressible comfort of feeling safe with a person having neither to weigh thoughts nor measure words, but to pour them all out, just as they are, chaff and grain together, knowing that a faithful hand will take and sift them, keep what is worth keeping, and then, with the breath of kindness, blow the rest away.

~George Eliot

The ABCs of Friends Are...

*A*mazing, cherish them

*B*lessings, acknowledge them

*C*aring, allow them

*D*ependable, rely on them

*E*ncouraging, hear them

*F*allible, love them

*G*ifts, unwrap them

*H*ealing, be with them

*I*mportant, value them

*J*uicy, savor them

*K*ind, delight in them

*L*oyal, mirror them

*M*agical, soar with them

*N*ecessary, cultivate them

*O*ptimistic, support them

*P*riceless, treasure them

*Q*uirky, enjoy them

*R*are, hold on to them

*S*trong, lean on them

*T*eachers, learn from them

*U*nderstanding, talk to them

*V*ulnerable, embrace them

*W*armhearted, listen to them

*X*traordinary, recognize them

*Y*oung at heart, play with them

*Z*any, laugh with them

©Meiji Stewart

Dare to…Make New Friends

*There is a magnet in your heart that will attract true friends.
That magnet is unselfishness, thinking of others first.
When you learn to live for others, they will live for you.*

~Paramahansa Yogananda

*A friend is someone who knows your song,
and sings it to you when you forget.*

~Eric Spiess

Dare to...

Nurture
Your Spirit

Dare to…Nurture Your Spirit

I still find each day too short for all the thoughts I want to think, all the walks I want to take, all the books I want to read, and all the friends I want to see. The longer I live, the more my mind dwells upon the beauty and the wonder of the world.

~John Burroughs

Happiness is when what you think, what you say, and what you do are in harmony.

~Mahatma Gandhi

Dare to…Nurture Your Spirit

*Though we travel the world over to find the beautiful,
we must carry it with us or we find it not.*

~Ralph Waldo Emerson

*For just a brief while every day
I steal away from duty
And leave the indoor tasks undone
To keep a tryst with beauty.*

~Mary Scott Fitzgerald

Dare to…Nurture Your Spirit

Stop doing anything unless your pure motive in doing it is to serve life. Now, that's a pretty radical concept. It's pretty hard to even imagine just doing things because it's play, and it will be play if your sole reason is to enrich life. But if we look at that to the degree to which we create our lives so that we are doing things solely out of a desire to enrich life, and not to avoid punishment, to avoid guilt, to avoid shame, out of a vague sense of obligation and duty, to the degree to which moment by moment we see life as playfulness of serving life, to that degree we are being compassionate to ourselves.

~Marshall B. Rosenberg

*Prayer is the peace of our spirit, the stillness of our thoughts,
the evenness of our recollection, the sea of our meditation,
the rest of our cares, and the calm of our tempest.*

~Jeremy Taylor

*There are four things in which every man must interest
himself. Who am I? Wherefore have I come from?
Whither am I going? How long shall I be here?
All spiritual inquiry begins with these questions and
attempts to find out the answers.*

~Diana Baskin

Dare to…Nurture Your Spirit

The Indian sees no need for setting apart one day in seven as holy day, since to him all days are Gods'.

~Charles E. Eastman

We need to find God, and he cannot be found in noise and restlessness. God is the friend of silence.

~Mother Teresa

Dare to...

Overcome
Adversity

*No man is more unhappy than the one who is never in adversity;
the greatest affliction of life is never to be afflicted.*

~Author unknown

*To succeed in any endeavor takes relentless belief in yourself.
We have to be committed. We can determine our destiny.*

~Willye B. White

The ABCs of Don't Quit...

Anything can happen.

Bend don't break.

Challenge your potential.

Destiny is a choice.

Effort creates opportunities.

Fly in the face of adversity.

Get back up and try again.

Hold on to your vision.

Impress yourself.

Just dig a little deeper.

Keep knocking on doors.

Learn from mistakes.

Motivate with compassion.

Nothing worthwhile comes easy.

Own a positive attitude.

Problems hold messages.

Question what's not working.

Regroup when you need to.

Shoot for the moon.

Think outside the box.

Understand "This too shall pass."

Value knowing when to walk away.

Work smarter not harder.

Xhaust all possibilities.

You can if you think you can.

Zest to do your best.

©*Meiji Stewart*

Dare to…Overcome Adversity

> *Adversity has the effect of eliciting talents which in prosperous circumstances would have lain dormant.*
>
> ~Horace

> *Our greatest glory is not in never failing but in rising every time we fail.*
>
> ~Ralph Waldo Emerson

> *It is not because things are difficult that we do not dare; it is because we do not dare that they are difficult.*
>
> ~Lucius Annaeus Seneca

Dare to…Overcome Adversity

We who lived in concentration camps can remember the men who walked through the huts comforting others, giving away their last piece of bread. They may have been few in number, but they offer sufficient proof that everything can be taken from a man but one thing: the last of human freedoms—to choose one's attitude in any given set of circumstances.

~Victor Frankl

Dare to…Overcome Adversity

> *People are always blaming their circumstances
> for what they are. I don't believe in circumstances.
> The people who get on in this world are the people
> who get up and look for the circumstances they want,
> and if they can't find them, make them.*
>
> ~George Bernard Shaw

> *The marvelous richness of human experience
> would lose something of rewarding joy
> if there were not limitations to overcome.*
>
> ~Helen Keller

Dare to...

Play

More

Dare to…Play More

The real joy of life is in its play. . . . Anything we do for the joy and love of doing it.

~Walter Raughenbusch

Learn some and think some and draw and paint and sing and dance and play and work some every day.

~Robert Fulghum

Dare to…Play More

Don't do anything that isn't play.
When our soul energy behind any action is simply to make life
wonderful for others and ourselves, then even hard work has
an element of play to it, joy to it, because we see that what we
are doing is for life serving purposes. These same efforts, if
they are mixed in to any degree with doing it out of
obligation, duty, fear, guilt, shame, the very action which
otherwise could come from play, a joy, now is something that
we don't like doing. We will resist doing.

~Marshall B. Rosenberg

Dare to…Play More

People who never get carried away should be.

~Malcolm Forbes

*Don't worry about the world coming to an end today.
It's already tomorrow in Australia.*

~Charles Schulz

*When faced with a decision, I always ask,
"What would be the most fun?"*

~Peggy Walker

*There is nothing more remarkable in the life of Socrates
than that he found time in his old age to learn to dance and play
on instruments, and thought it was time well spent.*

~Michel de Montaigne

Do not take life too seriously. You will never get out of it alive.

~Elbert Hubbard

Lose your sense of humor and you are truly lost.

~Ethan McCarty

Dare to…Play More

*The purpose of play is to go out and be happy…
to lay down cares and have fun for a while.*

~William Dorn

If you obey all the rules you miss all the fun.

~Katharine Hepburn

No, you never get any fun out of things you haven't done.

~Ogden Nash

Dare to...

Question
Conformity

Dare to…Question Conformity

The important thing is not to stop questioning.

~Albert Einstein

Read, every day, something no one else is reading.
Think, every day, something no one else is thinking.
Do, every day, something no one else would be silly enough to do.
It is bad for the mind to continually be part of unanimity.

~Christopher Morley

Dare to…Question Conformity

*Whenever you find yourself on the side of the majority,
it is time to pause and reflect.*

~Mark Twain

*I believe in rules. Sure I do.
If there weren't any rules, how could you break them?*

~Leo Durocher

*Creativity is inventing, experimenting, growing, taking risks,
breaking rules, making mistakes, and having fun.*

~Mary Lou Cook

Dare to…Question Conformity

*How far would Moses have gone
if he had taken a poll in Egypt?*

~Harry S. Truman

*It is better to ask some questions
than to know all the answers.*

~James Thurber

*Be who you are and say what you feel, because those who
mind don't matter and those who matter don't mind.*

~Dr. Seuss

Dare to…Question Conformity

Do not believe what you have heard.
Do not believe in tradition because it is handed down many generations.
Do not believe in anything that has been spoken of many times.
Do not believe because the written statements come from some old sage.
Do not believe in conjecture.
Do not believe in authority or teachers or elders.
But after careful observation and analysis,
when it agrees with reason and it will benefit one and all,
then accept it and live by it.

~Buddha

Dare to…Question Conformity

*Do not compare yourself with others,
for you are a unique and wonderful creation.
Make your own beautiful footprints in the snow.*

~Barbara Kimball

*The hallmark of courage in our age of conformity
is the capacity to stand on one's own convictions.*

~Rollo May

Dare to...

Reach
For The Stars

Dare to…Reach For The Stars

> *If we did the things we are capable of,*
> *we would astound ourselves.*
>
> ~Thomas Edison

> *Each day affirm that there is nothing in this world*
> *that can stop you from transforming your life,*
> *opening your heart, loving yourself,*
> *and sharing your love with everyone you encounter.*
>
> ~Yogi Amrit Desai

Dare to…Reach For The Stars

Did you ever hear of a man who had striven all his life faithfully and singly toward an object, and in no measure obtained it? If a man constantly aspires, is he not elevated?

~Henry David Thoreau

You seldom get what you go after unless you know in advance what you want.

~Maurice Switzer

Dare to…Reach For The Stars

*There are those of us who are always about to live.
We are waiting until things change, until there is more time,
until we are less tired, until we get a promotion,
until we settle down–until, until, until.
It always seems as if there is some major event
that must occur in our lives before we begin living.*

~George Sheehan

*Whatever you want to do, do it now.
There are only so many tomorrows.*

~Michael Landon

The ABCs of Success Are...

*A*ttitude, more than aptitude.

*B*eing happy with who you are.

*C*ultivating, body, mind, and spirit.

*D*iscovering, that heaven is within.

*E*mbracing, the unknown with enthusiasm.

*F*acing fear, finding faith.

*G*iving, without remembering.

*H*ere now, breathe into each moment.

*I*nside you, not in people, places, or things.

*J*ourneying, from the head to the heart.

*K*nowing, your beliefs create your experiences.

*L*etting go, and going with the flow.

*M*aking time, for family, friends, and forgiveness.

*N*ever ever giving up, on your hopes and dreams.

*O*pening your heart, to magnificent possibilities.

*P*assion, playfulness, and peace of mind.

*Q*uiet time, the key to inspired living.

*R*eceiving, without forgetting.

*S*eeking answers, questioning beliefs.

*T*rusting, in the beauty of your feelings and needs.

*U*nderstanding, the best you can do is always enough.

*V*erb, choreograph your dance with destiny.

*W*illingness, to learn from everything that happens.

*X*pressing yourself, be the hero of your own story.

*Y*ours to define, how do you want to be remembered?

*Z*estful living, loving, and laughing.

©*Meiji Stewart*

*Far away there in the sunshine are my highest aspirations.
I may not reach them, but I can look up and see their beauty,
believe in them and try to follow where they may lead.*

~Louisa May Alcott

*There are many wonderful things that will never be done
if you do not do them.*

~Charles D. Gill

Dare to...

Speak
Your Truth

Dare to…Speak Your Truth

Speak your truth, the answers will come.

~Marshall B. Rosenberg

The most exhausting thing in life is being insincere.

~Anne Morrow Lindbergh

I speak truth, not so much as I would,
but as much as I dare;
and I dare a little more as I grow older.

~Michel de Montaigne

*It is not the number of books you read,
nor the variety of sermons you hear,
but it is the frequency and earnestness with which you
meditate on these things till the truth in them becomes your
own and part of your being, that ensures your growth.*

~F. W. Robertson

*Say not "I have found the truth," but rather
"I have found a truth."*

~Khalil Gibran

Dare to…Speak Your Truth

> *Whenever you are to do a thing, though it can never be known but to yourself, ask yourself how you would act were all the world looking at you, and act accordingly.*
>
> ~Thomas Jefferson

> *When we become conditioned to perceived truth and closed to new possibilities, the following happens:*
> *We see what we expect to see, not what we can see.*
> *We hear what we expect to hear, not what we can hear.*
> *We think what we expect to think, not what we can think.*
>
> ~John Maxwell

Dare to…Speak Your Truth

*It's important that people know what you stand for.
It's equally important that they know what you won't stand for.*

~Mary Waldrop

*"Hush, don't say that–you'll lose some of your friends."
My answer is simple and final:
if I don't say it, I'll lose my own soul.*

~E. Stanley Jones

Dare to…Speak Your Truth

> *Observing without evaluating is the highest form of human intelligence.*
>
> ~Jiddu Krishnamurti

> *"Observe!! There are few things as important, as religious, as that."*
>
> ~Frederick Buechner

> *For most of us, it is difficult to make observations of people and their behavior that are free of judgment, criticism, or other forms of analysis.*
>
> ~Marshall B. Rosenberg

Dare to...

Take *Personal Responsibility*

You are the architect of your personal experience.

~Shirley MacLaine

This is a story about four people named Everybody, Somebody, Anybody, and Nobody. There was an important job to be done and Everybody was sure that Somebody would do it. Anybody could have done it, but Nobody did it. Somebody got angry about that, because it was Everybody's job. Everybody thought Anybody could do it, but Nobody realized that Everybody wouldn't do it. It ended up that Everybody blamed Somebody when Nobody did what Anyone could have done.

~Author unknown

Dare to…Take Personal Responsibility

If you don't like the scene you're in, if you are unhappy, if you're lonely, if you don't feel that things are happening, change your scene. Paint a new backdrop. Surround yourself with new actors. Write a new play— and if it's not a good play, get off the stage and write another one. There are millions of plays—as many as there are people.

~Leo Buscaglia

The willingness to accept responsibility for one's own life is the source from which self-respect springs.

~Joan Didion

Dare to…Take Personal Responsibility

*Life is not the way it's supposed to be. It's the way it is.
The way you cope with it is what makes the difference.*

~Virginia Satir

*Experience is determined by yourself—
not the circumstances of your life.*

~Gita Bellin

*Stop looking for a scapegoat in your life, be willing to face the
truth within yourself, and right your own wrongs.*

~Eileen Caddy

What others say and do may be the stimulus, but never the cause of our feelings. We see that our feelings result from how we choose to receive what others say and do, as well as our particular needs and expectations in that moment.

~Marshall B. Rosenberg

We create our own feelings by the thoughts we choose to think. We have the ability to make different choices and create different experiences.

~Louise Hay

Dare to…Take Personal Responsibility

*What we are today comes from our thoughts of yesterday,
and our present thoughts build our life of tomorrow:
Our life is the creation of our mind.*

~Buddha

*If not you, then who?
If not now, then when?*

~Hillel

Dare to...

Understand More, *Judge Less*

Dare to…Understand More, Judge Less

If you judge people, you have no time to love them.

~Mother Teresa

*It is understanding that gives us an ability to have peace.
When we understand the other fellow's viewpoint,
and he understands ours, then we can sit down
and work out our differences.*

~Harry S. Truman

Dare to…Understand More, Judge Less

*If we could read the secret history of our enemies,
we should find in each man's life sorrow and suffering
enough to disarm all hostility.*

~Henry Wadsworth Longfellow

*If someone listens, or stretches out a hand,
or whispers a kind word of encouragement,
or attempts to understand a lonely person,
extraordinary things begin to happen.*

~Loretta Garzartis

Dare to…Understand More, Judge Less

There is no right or wrong. There is only opinion.

~A. J. Carothers

Do not weep; do not wax indignant. Understand.

~Baruch Spinoza

You never really understand a person until you consider things from their point of view.

~Harper Lee

Dare to…Understand More, Judge Less

*The motto should not be, "forgive one another;"
rather, "Understand one another."*

~Emma Goldman

*Whenever we imply that someone else is wrong in some way,
we are really saying that that person is not acting in harmony
with our needs.*

~Marshall B. Rosenberg

Dare to…Understand More, Judge Less

> *When…someone really hears you without passing judgment on you, without trying to take responsibility for you, without trying to mold you, it feels good.*
>
> ~Carl Rogers

> *Out beyond ideas of wrongdoing and rightdoing, there is a field. I will meet you there.*
>
> ~Rumi

Dare to...

Volunteer
Your Time

Dare to…Volunteer Your Time

The only ones among you who will be really happy are those who will have sought and found how to serve.

~Albert Schweitzer

Only a life in the service of others is worth living.

~Albert Einstein

Dare to…Volunteer Your Time

*Many persons have a wrong idea of what constitutes real happiness.
It is not obtained through self-gratification,
but through fidelity to a worthy purpose.*

~Helen Keller

*Giving is a joy if we do it in the right spirit.
It all depends on whether we think of it as
"What can I spare?" or as "What can I share?"*

~Esther York Burkholder

Dare to…Volunteer Your Time

> *We make a living by what we get,*
> *but we make a life by what we give.*
>
> ~Henry Bucher

> *Nobody could make a greater mistake*
> *than he who did nothing because*
> *he could only do a little.*
>
> ~Edmund Burke

*The purpose of life is to matter—
to count, to stand for something,
to have it make some difference that we lived at all.*

~Leo Rosten

Giving opens the way for receiving.

~Florence Scovel Shinn

*I have found that there is a tremendous joy in giving.
It is a very important part of the joy of living.*

~William Black

Dare to…Volunteer Your Time

G*oodness is the only investment that never fails.*

~Henry David Thoreau

Y*ou will find, as you look back upon your life,*
that the moments that stand out
are the moments when you have done things for others.

~Henry Drummond

Dare to...

Walk
Through Fear

What is needed, rather than running away or controlling or suppressing or any other resistance, is understanding fear; that means, watch it, learn about it, come directly into contact with it. We are to learn about fear, not how to escape from it.

~Jiddu Krishnamurti

Fear is a question: What are you afraid of, and why? Just as the seed of health is in illness, because illness contains information, your fears are a treasure house of self-knowledge if you explore them.

~Marilyn Ferguson

Dare to…Walk Through Fear

*We were born to make manifest the glory of
God that is within us. It's not just in some
of us, it is in everyone.
And as we let our own light shine, we
unconsciously give other people permission
to do the same.
As we are liberated from our fear, our
presence automatically liberates others.*

~Marianne Williamson

If you wait until you're ready, you'll wait forever.

~Will Rogers

Listen to your fear with a wise ear.
What are you afraid of in life?
What are you afraid of in yourself?
You must challenge fear and ask it what it means to say.

~Emmanuel's Book

Fear of failure brings fear of taking risks ...
and you're never going to get what you want out of life
without taking some risks. Remember, everything worthwhile
carries the risk of failure.

~Lee Iacocca

We lose much by fearing to attempt.

~J. N. Moffit

Take a chance! All life is a chance. The person who goes farthest is generally the one who is willing to do and dare. The "sure thing" boat never gets far from shore.

~Dale Carnegie

Dare to…Walk Through Fear

*The moment you commit and quit holding back,
all sorts of unforeseen incidents, meetings and material
assistance will rise up to help you. The simple act of
commitment is a powerful magnet for help.*

~Napoleon Hill

*One of the greatest discoveries a man makes,
one of his great surprises,
is to find he can do what he was afraid he couldn't do.*

~Henry Ford

Dare to...

Xperience
The Moment

Every morning is a fresh beginning.
Every day is the world made new.
Today is a new day.
Today is my world made new.
This is my day of opportunity.

~Dan Custer

To be concentrated means to live fully in the present,
in the here and now, and not to think of the next thing to be done,
while I am doing something right now.

~Erich Fromm

Each second we live is a unique moment of the universe—a moment that never was before and will never be again.

~Pablo Casals

To stay in touch with life's sweet flow, is moment by moment to stay connected to how we are at that moment. What does that mean? To me, that means getting connected to how we're feeling. And what we're needing. When I can be in touch with that in myself, I feel alive, I feel I'm in touch with life's sweet flow when I'm in touch with the feelings and the needs going on in other people.

~Marshall B. Rosenberg

Dare to…Xperience The Moment

> *In spite of all similarities, every living situation has, like a newborn child, a new face that has never been before and will never come again. It demands of you a reaction that cannot be prepared beforehand. It demands nothing of what is past. It demands presence, responsibility; it demands you.*
>
> ~Martin Buber

> *Today a new sun rises for me, everything lives, everything is animated, everything seems to speak to me of my passion, everything invites me to cherish it.*
>
> ~Anne de Lenclos

Dare to...

Yearn

For Grace

Through many dangers, toils, and snares we have already come; 'Twas grace that brought us safe thus far, and grace will lead us home.

~John Newton

You say grace before meals. All right. But I say grace before the concert and the opera, and grace before the play and pantomime, and grace before I open a book, and grace before sketching, painting, swimming, fencing, boxing, walking, playing, dancing and grace before I dip the pen in the ink.

~G. K. Chesterton

Dare to…Yearn For Grace

The grace of God means something like:
Here is your life. You might never have been,
but you are because the party
wouldn't have been complete without you.
Here is the world. Beautiful and terrible things will happen.
Don't be afraid. I am with you. Nothing can ever separate us.
It's for you I created the universe. I love you.

~Frederick Buechner

Where are you searching for me, friend? Look!
Here I am right within you.
Not in temple, nor in mosque, not in Kaaba,
nor Kailas, but here within you I am.

~Kabir

Dare to…Yearn For Grace

> *How often things occur by mere chance*
> *which we dare not even hope for.*
>
> ~Terence

> *God grant me the serenity*
> *to accept the things I cannot change,*
> *the courage to change the things I can,*
> *and the wisdom to know the difference.*
>
> ~Reinhold Niebuhr

Dare to...

be Zany

Dare to…be Zany

Life is too important to be taken seriously.

~Oscar Wilde

My advice to you is not to inquire why or whither, but just enjoy your ice cream while it's on your plate– that's my philosophy.

~Thornton Wilder

The ABCs of Life Are Too Short to…

*A*lways "play it safe."

*B*e "right" instead of happy.

*C*ompare yourself to others.

*D*o "just enough" to get by.

*E*ngage your mouth when angry.

*F*orget what's really important.

*G*ive up on your dreams.

*H*ave a chip on your shoulder.

*I*ndulge in extremes.

*J*ust work for the money.

*K*eep walking on eggshells.

*L*ook outside for answers.

*M*ake mountains out of molehills.

*N*ot learn from your mistakes.

*O*bey all of the rules.

*P*retend to be someone you're not.

*Q*uit when the going gets tough.

*R*isk nothing, do nothing, be nothing.

*S*top asking questions.

*T*ry to please everybody.

*U*se blame, shame, or guilt.

*V*alue things more than people.

*W*ait for the other shoe to drop.

*X*perience life as a spectator.

*Y*earn for the "good old days."

*Z*ip right through it.

©Meiji Stewart

Dare to…be Zany

Be brave enough to live creatively. The creative is the place where no one else has ever been. You have to leave the city of your comfort and go into the wilderness of your intuition. You can't get there by bus, only by hard work, risking, and by not quite knowing what you're doing. What you'll discover will be wonderful: yourself.

~Alan Alda

Why go into something to test the waters? Go into it to make waves.

~Michael Nolan

Little ABC gift books, big messages

#1871

#1872

Stay in touch with those you love and care about by sending a unique
ABC writing eCard for just about every occasion from *www.abcecards.com*

To order these great gift books, call 1-800-328-9000 or go to *www.hazelden.org/bookplace*

Little gift books, big messages

#8313

#6608

#6456

#6460

To order these great gift books, call 1-800-328-9000 or go to *www.hazelden.org/bookplace*

Little gift books, big messages

#6458 — It's a Jungle Out There! Be kind to fellow travelers.

#6568 — Parenting... Part Joy... Part Guerrilla Warfare. Celebrating the delights and challenges of parenting

#6569 — God Danced the Day You Were Born. Humor & wisdom for celebrating life

#6566 — Happiness is an Inside Job. Humor & wisdom celebrating the art of happiness

To order these great gift books, call 1-800-328-9000 or go to *www.hazelden.org/bookplace*

Little gift books, big messages

#6457 — Children are Meant to be Seen & Heard — humor and wisdom for honoring children

#6570 — Anything is Possible — Humor & wisdom for success and prosperity

#1737 — Follow Your Dreams — You can if you think you can

#1736 — Friends — May you always have loving friendships

To order these great gift books, call 1-800-328-9000 or go to *www.hazelden.org/bookplace*

ABOUT THE AUTHOR
MEIJI STEWART

Meiji has created gift books, designs, and writings that may be of interest to you. Please visit *www.puddledancer.com* or call 1-858-759-6963 for more information. Thank you.

(1) **ABC WRITINGS** - *27 ABC titles and gift products are available to view at www.abcwritings.com. Stay in touch with those you love and care about by sending a unique ABC writing eCard for just about every occasion from www.abcecards.com. Many of these ABC writings are available as posters (from Portal Publications) at your favorite poster and gift store, or on a variety of gift products from Hazelden.*

(2) **KEEP COMING BACK** - *over 200 gift products including: gift books, greeting cards, wallet cards, bookmarks, magnets, bumper stickers, and more. Free catalog available from Hazelden at 1-800-328-9000 or view products at www.hazelden.org/bookplace.*

(3) **NONVIOLENT COMMUNICATION: A LANGUAGE OF COMPASSION** by Marshall B. Rosenberg (from PuddleDancer Press) - *Jack Canfield (*Chicken Soup for the Soul *author) says, "I believe the principles and techniques in this book can literally change the world–but more importantly, they can change the quality of your life with your spouse, your children, your neighbors, your co-workers, and everyone else you interact with. I cannot recommend it highly enough." Available from Hazelden and your local and on-line bookstores. Visit **www.nonviolentcommunication.com**.*

For more information about the Center for Nonviolent Communication (CNVC) call 1-800-255-7696 or visit *www.cnvc.org.*

HAZELDEN

Keep Coming Back

Complimentary Catalog Available
Hazelden, P.O. Box 176, Center City, MN 55012-0176
1-800-328-9000   www.hazelden.org

Hazelden/Keep Coming Back titles available from your favorite bookstore:

The ABCs of Dare to...	ISBN 1-56838-744-X
The ABCs of May You Always Have...	ISBN 1-56838-745-8
Relax, God Is in Charge	ISBN 1-56838-377-0
Keep Coming Back	ISBN 1-56838-378-9
Children Are Meant to Be Seen and Heard	ISBN 1-56838-379-7
Shoot for the Moon	ISBN 1-56838-380-0
When Life Gives You Lemons…	ISBN 1-56838-381-9
It's a Jungle Out There!	ISBN 1-56838-382-7
Parenting...Part Joy...Part Guerrilla Warfare	ISBN 1-56838-383-5
God Danced the Day You Were Born	ISBN 1-56838-384-3
Happiness Is an Inside Job	ISBN 1-56838-385-1
Anything Is Possible	ISBN 1-56838-386-X
Follow Your Dreams	ISBN 1-56838-514-5
Friends	ISBN 1-56838-515-3

Acknowledgments

Every effort has been made to find the copyright owner of the material used. However, there are a few quotations that have been impossible to trace, and we would be glad to hear from the copyright owners of these quotations so that acknowledgment can be recognized in any future edition.